HORSE
CARE
RIDING & TRAINING

Elaine Heney

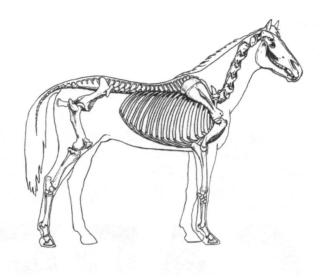

"We begin by listening to the horse"

Elaine Heney

GUESS THE WORDS

I		_	O	U	_
H	_	R	_	E	S

THIS BOOK
BELONGS TO

_____

Children's books by Elaine Heney

www.elaineheneybooks.com

Listenology for Kids
Horse Care for Kids
The Forgotten Horse
The Show Horse
The Mayfield Horse
The Stolen Horse
The Adventure Horse
The Lost Horse

Saddlestone Pony Listening School

Sinead and Strawberry
Roisin and Rhubarb
Conor and Coconut
Fiona and Foxtrot
The Saddlestone Quiz Book

Other books by Elaine Heney

Equine Listenology Guide
Dressage for Beginners
Listenology Guide to Bitless Bridles
The Horse Anatomy Coloring Book
Conversations with the Horse

Horse Riding Apps

www.horsestridesapp.com
www.rideableapp.com
www.dressagehero.com
www.greyponyfilms.com

Online courses

www.greyponyfilms.com

TABLE OF CONTENTS

 What do you call a noisy horse?
A herd animal.

INTRODUCTION

Horses are amazing animals. When you fall in love with horses you will want to learn everything about them. All horses have feelings and are unique, just like us!

Some horses are funny, others are serious. Some are goofy, others are very sweet. Some like to take it easy and are economical. Other horses tend to be in a hurry and like to go fast. They all have their own personalities! Horses can be very big, but they are also very sensitive.

Even though horses don't "speak" with words, they have many ways of communicating. They have a very good memory, so it is very important that we always treat them kindly and do our best to understand their point of view. Horses have their own special language, which you can learn. One of the best things about horses is that they are honest, and a horse will never lie. It's our job to learn as much as we can about our horses, so we can understand them better.

 Did you know: Horses are very social animals & make strong friendships with other horses.

CONNECT EACH HORSE TO THE CORRECT SHADOW

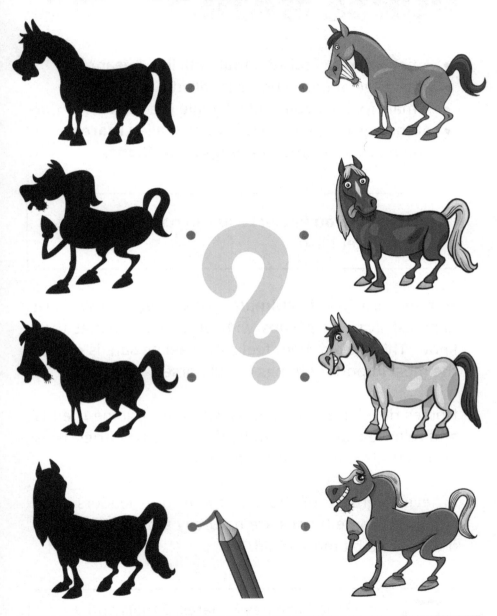

HORSE NAMES

- A baby horse is called a **foal** until it is 1 year old.
- At the age of one, a horse is called a **yearling**.
- A male foal is a **colt** and a female is a **filly**.
- At the age of 4, female horses are called **mares**, and males are either **geldings or stallions**.

Did you know: Foals can run within hours after birth.

Horses are herd animals. This means they are happiest living in groups with other horses that they know. This makes them feel safe. Feeling safe is one of the most important things for all horses.

Horses develop strong bonds with their equine friends and relatives. Just like people, they have best friends as well as dislikes for certain other horses.

In every group of horses there are leaders and followers. Some horses are naturally a bit bossy, whilst others are a bit more timid.

If a stud farm has 6 mares, 6 foals and 3 stallions, how many horses do they have?

Answer: 15 horses

Do you know the difference between a horse and a pony?

Horses and ponies are measured in hands. One hand is the same as 4 inches. A horse is over 14.2 hands. A pony is 14.2 hands or smaller.

 Did you know: On average, most domesticated horses live until they are around 25 to 30 years old. Some horses can live to be over 30 or 40 years of age.

Old age & horses.

Just like people, we need to look after our horses' health all their lives. When we train our horse slowly, and look after their bodies, many horses can still be healthy & perfect to ride well into their 20's and even into their 30's!

We must always take care of our horses so they can be ridden for many years to come, in good health.

Horses can live until they are in their 30's or even 40's. One of the oldest horses in the world was Sugar Puff who lived until he was 56 years old.

HANDWRITING CHALLENGE

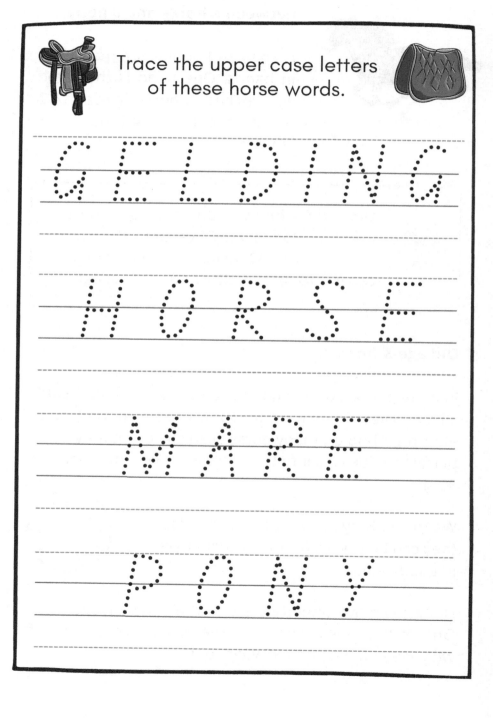

Trace the upper case letters
of these horse words.

GELDING

HORSE

MARE

PONY

HORSE BEHAVIOUR

A horse's behaviour has a lot to do with being a prey animal. Some animals, such as humans, lions and tigers are predators. In nature, predators eat prey animals. Prey animals, like horses, have a very strong instinct to look out for and run from danger so they don't get eaten!

This is why horses have a very strong need to feel safe in their herd. Horses also want to feel safe when they are with you. When horses don't feel safe, they can spend a lot of time looking out for danger.

If you watch a herd of horses closely you will see that they take turns standing guard. You may see one or more horses having a nap, while one horse keeps watch. When horses don't feel safe, their first instinct is to run very fast.

To show them that we are their friends instead of predators, it's important that we try to communicate with them in the way they understand. Even though they don't use words, horses have a very special language of their own - body language!

 If we are feeling sad or angry the horses can see this instantly in our body without us telling them!

HORSE BODY LANGUAGE

Horses communicate mostly with body language. Instead of words, they use movement to talk to each other. Learning how horses use body language with each other helps us to understand what they are saying and how they are feeling. It also helps us to talk to them in a way that they understand.

Some of these movements may be really small:

- A flick of an ear might mean a horse has just heard something, it might mean he is irritated, it might also mean he is paying attention.
- The slightest lowering of the head might mean a horse is starting a nap, but it might show that he is wanting you or another horse to move out of his space.
- A tiny wrinkling of the nostrils might mean he is concentrating hard, but might also mean he is getting worried.

Other movements might be much bigger, such as:

- A tail swish could mean there is a fly buzzing around, or another horse is getting too close.
- Biting and kicking are really big movements. Horses save these for when they feel their smaller movements haven't been noticed. We can do this too. Just like our horses, when we are asking them to do something, we should ask with a small cue first.

Even though we move and look like predators, by showing horses that we understand their language we can help them feel confident around us.

MAZE! HELP YOUR HORSE FIND HIS FRIENDS

Start here

BONDING WITH YOUR HORSE

To bond with your horse you must learn his language and also his own personal likes and dislikes. You will also need to become a confident partner and leader.

Leadership doesn't mean you have to be bossy!

It means you have to always be **fair, patient and kind.** You have to find out how to get your horse to believe that you will always keep him safe, even when you ask for things that your horse doesn't understand or finds scary.

 When does a horse talk? Whinny wants to!

Most horses accept being cuddled once they know you, but it may not be important for them. Your horse may prefer to be scratched on the neck, or on the withers or his back.

At first, when you are getting to know each other, don't rush and try to pat all over your horse's face. You wouldn't like that and neither do horses. It feels much nicer if you offer them a gentle rub. Don't force anything, go slow & be patient when bonding with your horse.

 Did you know: When horses look like they're laughing, they're actually engaging in a special nose-enhancing technique known as "flehmen," to determine whether a smell is good or bad.

When you are with your horse, you must always remember that his feelings matter as much as your own, and maybe even more because the horse has less choice about it than you do.

It's your job to try and see how he feels about what you want and find ways to make your horse want to be with you and do the things you like.

The very first step in bonding with your horse is to speak to him in his own language.

Once a horse sees that you are paying attention to what he is saying, even if you make mistakes, he will try harder to communicate with you and enjoy being with you.

You are visiting your local tack shop. You buy a hoofpick for $3, a set of stirrups for $25 and a riding hat for $50. How much change do you get from $100?

Answer: $22

9 WAYS TO BOND WITH YOUR HORSE

- Always be kind with your horse.
- Never lose your patience or hit your horse or pony.
- Always feed & water your pony before you feed & water yourself. This can mean early mornings, late nights & looking after your horse in the snow & rain.

- Talk to your horse regularly and tell them how much you appreciate him/her.
- Look at life from your horse's perspective.
- Instead of 'making' your horse do things, ask yourself how you can 'help' your horse to do things.
- Break 1 big goal down into lots of tiny tasks. This strategy is called 'Eating the Elephant'.

How do you eat an elephant? One bite at a time!

- Manage your emotions around your horse. Be calm and predictable. Horses do not like noisy, loud or unpredictable people.
- Be a good and patient teacher.

GOOD TEACHER WORKSHEET

Think about one great teacher you have at school.
Write down all the reasons they are a good teacher.

1. ....

2. ....

3. ....

4. ....

5. ....

6. ....

7. ....

8. ....

9. ....

BONDING

Horses are very good at telling other horses to move away from them or allowing them to approach. Sometimes their movements are so small, it's hard for humans to see them.

- What does your horse do when you step towards him?
- Does he look away ever so slightly or even step away?
- Or does he immediately come towards you, even bump into you?

Respecting space is really important in horse language.

Approach and retreat exercise

If you have a horse that looks away, or lifts his head and gets very tense in his body, show him that you notice this by immediately backing away until he looks at you, or lowers his head back down. Then wait.

Maybe he'll lick and chew to show you that he appreciates you noticing.

Then walk towards him again a little more slowly and see if he still wants to look away. Try to stop and back away just before he does.

If you play this little game patiently enough, your horse will learn to trust that you are trying to speak his language. Maybe he will even get curious enough to walk towards you.

When you get good at this exercise, you will find it very useful with horses who don't like to come in from the field. You can also use it with grooming, tacking up and even to help him get brave about scary things.

Wait for him to touch your hand before you try to touch him. And if he looks away as you do, repeat the game, but this time with your hand. Reach with your hand, and take it away if he looks away from you.

"Forming a true relationship by getting to know your horse's personality, behaviours in different situations and his habits."

BONDING WITH YOUR HORSE

Make yourself bigger exercise

If you have a pushy horse who marches right up to you, and maybe even bumps into you, you can try making yourself a little bigger to move him out of your space. Just lift your arms up and down sideways. Not too fast! You're not trying to scare him or punish him. You're trying to make it clear that he's not noticed that he is too close. If he doesn't move, try moving your arms a little faster and if that doesn't work, bounce on the spot as well as moving your arms. When you get really good at this exercise, your horse will start to move away when all you do is THINK about making yourself bigger.

"The most important part of being around horses is staying safe. If you feel unsafe if a horse is coming towards you too fast, get out of there ASAP and ask an adult for help. Your safety always comes first.

End on a happy note

Try and find out what rewards your horse likes. Find out his favourite scratchy spots, and try to always stop before he needs you to. If you leave him wanting more, he'll remember how much he enjoyed it instead of wishing you'd stop it already! This is another great thing to learn about how horses think. If you always finish what you are doing together with something that makes him happy, he will look forward to the next time you are together.

HORSE BONDING QUIZ

1: Being a good leader means:

    a. Being bossy and shouting.
    b. Making sure my horse always does what I ask.
    c. Being patient and making sure my horse feels safe.
    d. Letting my horse do whatever he wants.

2: The most important part of being with horses is:

    a. Making the horse do what I want
    b. Riding my horse
    c. Teaching my horse new things
    d. Staying safe

3: The best way to cuddle a horse is to:

    a. Clap him really hard on the neck
    b. Use approach and retreat while finding his favourite scratching spots
    c. Throw my arms around his neck and tell him how much I love him
    d. Tie him up to stroke and groom him if he fidgets

4: If a horse walks away from me when I want to be with him I should:

    a. Show him that I noticed by stopping and taking a few steps back.
    b. Give up. He obviously hates me.
    c. Follow him until he understands I will never give up.
    d. Throw something at him so he knows how annoyed I am.

Answers: 1c, 2d, 3b, 4a

HORSE BREEDS

There are many horse & pony breeds around the world.

Shire

Percheron

Gypsy Vanner

Arab

Thoroughbred

Andalusian

Paint

Marwari

Akhal-Teke

Appaloosa

Fjord

Bashkir

Noriker

Shetland

Miniature

Horses come in all shapes and sizes. All breeds have distinct physical and temperamental characteristics because historically they had very particular jobs.

The big draft horses, like the Shire and Percheron horses, were bred for their strength and sensible personalities. They were used for pulling carts.

"While there's only one species of domestic horse, there are about **400 different breeds** around the world!"

Thoroughbreds are built for speed and are used for racing. Andalusian horses are very brave and were used for bullfighting.

SHETLAND PONY

Shetland ponies used to work in coal mines and also carried heavy loads to help farmers and gamekeepers in Scotland.

 Did you know: The world's smallest horse breed is the Falabella which ranges between 38-76 cm tall. They are called horses - even though they are pony size!

CAN YOU FIND FIVE HORSE BREEDS BELOW?

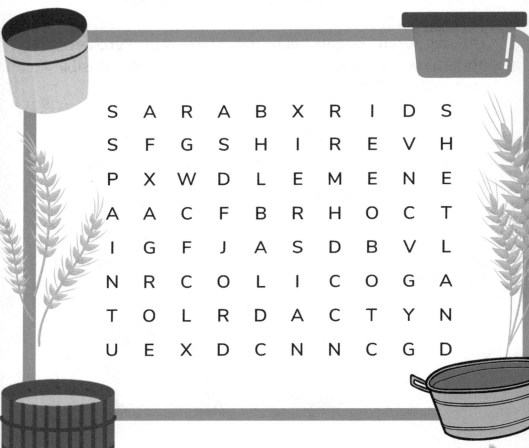

S A R A B X R I D S
S F G S H I R E V H
P X W D L E M E N E
A A C F B R H O C T
I G F J A S D B V L
N R C O L I C O G A
T O L R D A C T Y N
U E X D C N N C G D

FIND THE BREEDS QUIZ

FIND THESE WORDS: Shetland, Arab, Paint, Shire, Fjord

HORSE DISCIPLINES

 How can you tell a police horse from a normal horse? The police horse goes "Neigh-naw-neigh-naw-neigh-naw".

People have been using horses for all sorts of things for thousands of years. Horses were used in battle, on farms and for transportation. Now, most horses are kept for fun.

Some horses are still kept for work (police horses, guide ponies, forestry work). If you go to horse shows you will see horses who do eventing, showjumping, showing and dressage.

In the USA, western riding, barrel racing and reining are popular too.

More recently people are starting to do TREC and agility with their horses. There are also all kinds of racing competitions all over the world.

 What's the quickest way to mail a little horse? Use the Pony Express.

HORSE COLORS

Horses & ponies come in many different colours.

| Sorrel | Dapple grey | Bay | Blue dun |

| Grey | Flaxen chestnut | Skew-bald | Blue-eyed cream |

| Black | Dun | Liver chestnut | Red roan |

| Palomino | Appaloosa | Pie-bald | Buckskin |

How do you make a small fortune in the horse industry? Start with a large fortune

HORSE COLORS

Horses come in all sorts of shades, patterns and markings. The main colours are brown, bay, chestnut and grey.

A grey horse can be born nearly black and become lighter as it grows older until it is nearly white.

Some breeds always have specific colours (like the Friesian and the Fjord), and other breeds, like the Appaloosa are known for their spotted markings.

 Did you know: A white horse is called a grey horse. Most grey horses were a much darker colour when they were younger.

What street do horses live on? Mane St.

Horse Color

WORD SCRAMBLE

GUESS THE WORD!

RELSOR

YAB

NUTTHESC

PALDBIE

KABLC

 Why do horses like to fart when they buck? Because they can't achieve full horse power without gas.

Answers: Sorrel, Bay, Chestnut, Piebald, Black

Parts of the horse

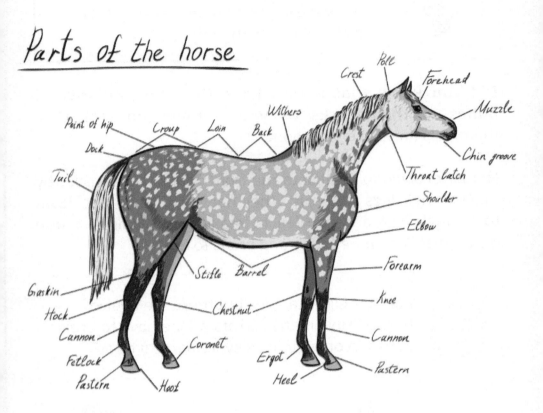

As a horse person, it's really valuable to know all of the parts of a horse's body. Take a moment & study the picture above. You'll need to know these names to improve your knowledge about horses!

 How long should a horse's legs be?
Long enough to reach the ground

HORSE ANATOMY

 Did you know: You can tell if a horse is cold by feeling behind their ears. If that area is cold, so is the horse.

Did you know that horses have the same number of bones in their necks as you? Giraffes do too! Most mammals have 7 cervical bones.

Horses evolved to be able to run from danger very quickly by making their legs very slim. They narrowed their feet down to a single toe on each leg to make them lighter. *It also makes their legs more fragile and prone to injury.*

 Karl has eight carrots, but there are twelve horses. How many carrots will he have to break in half in order to give every horse a treat?

4

 Did you know: Horses can only breathe through their nose, not through their mouth as humans can.

THE EQUINE SKELETON

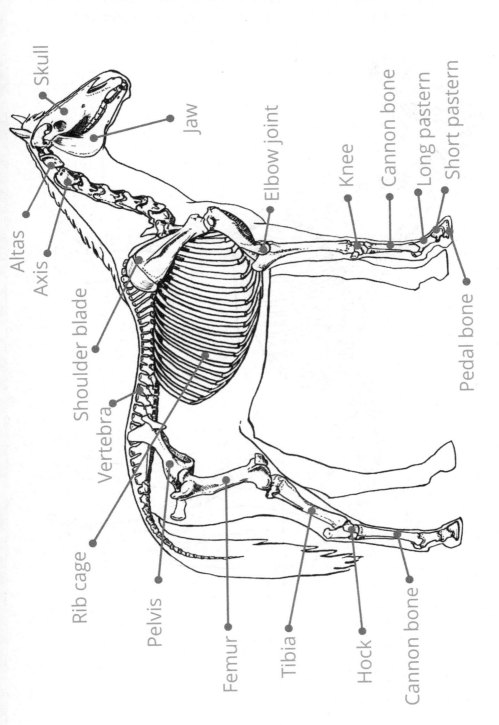

Skull

Jaw

Elbow joint

Knee

Cannon bone

Long pastern

Short pastern

Altas

Axis

Shoulder blade

Vertebra

Pedal bone

Rib cage

Pelvis

Femur

Tibia

Hock

Cannon bone

THE EQUINE SKELETON QUIZ

Test your knowledge of the equine skeleton

YOUR HORSE'S TEETH

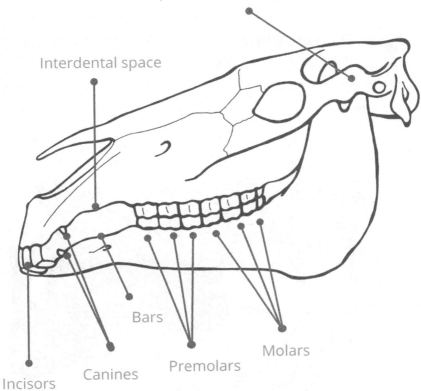

Temporomandibular joint

Interdental space

Incisors

Canines

Bars

Premolars

Molars

Horses' teeth need to be checked by an equine dentist **once or twice a year** to make sure they are wearing evenly. If they get sharp edges, they are filed down with a rasp.

You should always try to feed your horse from the ground because it helps the teeth line up properly and wear down evenly.

 Did you know: A horse's teeth take up a larger amount of space in their head than their brain.

YOUR HORSE'S TEETH

 Did you know: You can tell how old a horse is by looking at his teeth.

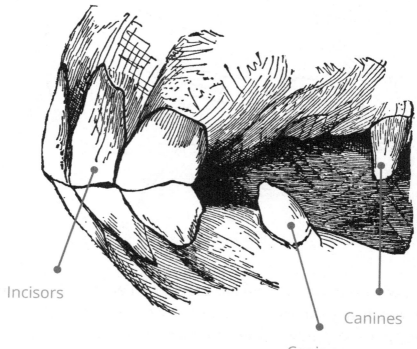

Incisors

Canines

Canines

 Interesting fact: The left side of your horse (often the side you mount on) is called the 'near' side. The right side is called the 'off' side.

YOUR HORSE'S FEET

Your horse's feet are called hooves. A horse's hooves grow all the time. Horse's hooves can get sore & uncomfortable if they are not trimmed regularly. They can get cracks & split, which is not good! As the old saying says: *No hoof, no horse!*

It's really important to always look after your horse's feet.

You will need to have the farrier trim your horse every 4-6 weeks to keep them comfortable. Lots of horses do not need to wear horse shoes. If your horse wears shoes, there should be a reason why - and not just because everyone else's horse does! Some horses without shoes wear boots on hard ground if they need them.

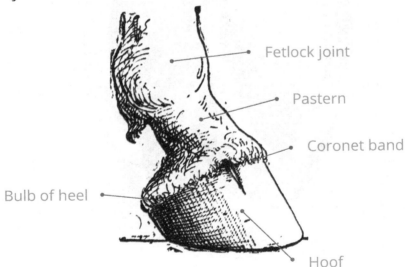

Fetlock joint

Pastern

Coronet band

Bulb of heel

Hoof

 Did you know: Horse hooves are made from the same protein that comprises human hair and fingernails.

YOUR HORSE'S FEET

Lift up your horse's hooves daily & pick out any dirt or small stones using a hoofpick. You use a hoofpick going from heel to toe. You do not use a hoofpick going from toe to heel.

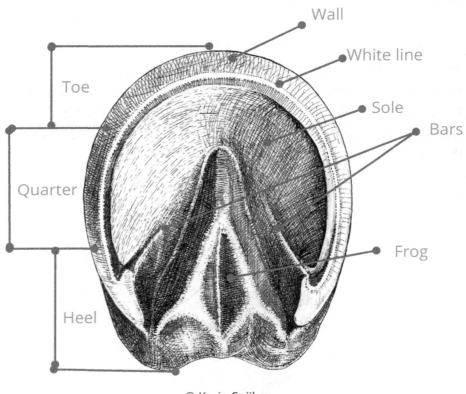

Wall

White line

Toe

Sole

Bars

Quarter

Frog

Heel

© Karin Spijker

 Did you know: It takes 9-12 months to re-grow an entire horse hoof.

HORSE ANATOMY CHALLENGE

F	E	T	L	O	C	K
N	E	A	G	A	E	N
H	A	I	D	L	E	E
O	G	L	R	T	H	E
O	O	O	I	E	A	L
F	I	H	O	C	K	E

Find 5 parts of the horse's body:

Fetlock – Knee – Hoof – Hock – Tail

HORSE PEOPLE

Vet: The vet is an animal doctor who will need to come and check your horse at least once a year and give him his flu and tetanus vaccinations. The vet will also help your horse if he gets sick.

Equine dentist: The dentist or horse vet will need to check your horse's teeth once or twice a year. If you are worried the bit may be hurting your horse's mouth, ask your dentist to check on their next visit.

Physiotherapist: The physio should check your horse for muscle pain if your horse is exercising hard, or there has been a change in how much work he does. Be sure to ask if there is any back pain, that may indicate there is a saddle fit issue. This needs to be checked on each visit.

Instructor(s): Even the best riders and trainers have lessons. It's a good idea to get help from good instructors to help you with your riding and groundwork. We never stop learning about horses - no matter what age we are!

Farrier: The farrier looks after your horse's feet, but you should also pick and brush them out thoroughly every single day, especially before riding!

Saddle fitter: You should have your saddle checked by a saddle fitter at least once a year. Your horse's shape can change very quickly.

HELP THE DENTIST FIND HER TOOLS

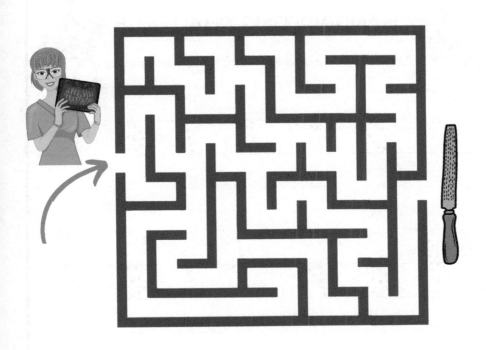

HELP THE VET FIND HIS CAR KEYS

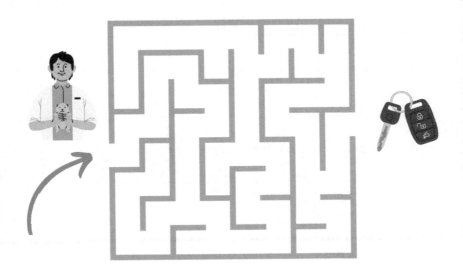

HANDWRITING CHALLENGE

Trace the lower case letters of these horse people

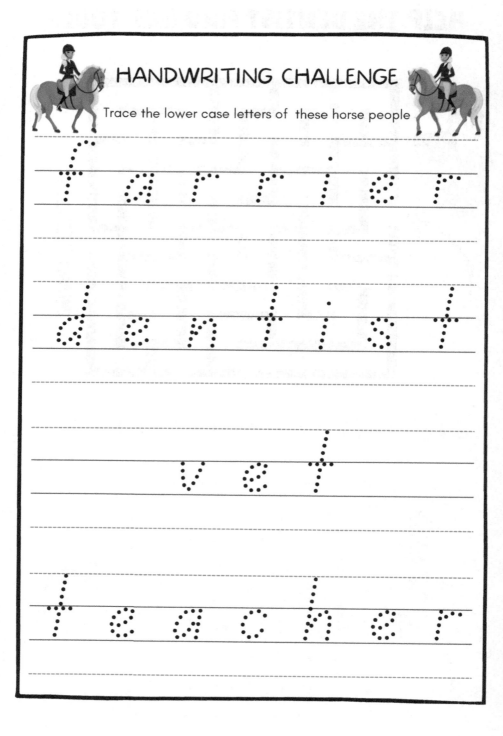

farrier

dentist

vet

teacher

HORSE PEOPLE QUIZ

1: When my horse is sick I will call the:

    a. Saddle fitter
    b. Dentist
    c. Vet
    d. Baker

2: When my horse has a sore tooth I will call the:

    a: Gardener
    b. Farrier
    c. Teacher.
    d. Equine dentist

3.When my horse has a sore foot I will call the:

    a. Farrier
    b. Physiotherapist
    c. Saddle fitter
    d. Fire brigade

4.When my horse has a sore back I will call the:

    a. Farrier
    b. Physiotherapist
    c. Equine dentist
    d. Instructor

Answers: 1c, 2d, 3a, 4b

YOUR HORSE'S HOME

Whether you keep your horse at home or at a barn or livery yard, all horses need:

Turnout with other horses. Horses are herd animals and must have other horses for company and **lots of space to move around.** It is not good for a horse's body to stand still all day.

Did you know: Horses can sleep lying down and standing up.

Shelter from the rain and wind. If your horse doesn't have a stable, make sure there is somewhere in the field where your horse can get out of the rain and wind, and never leave him to shiver. Perhaps some trees or a shelter. If your horse is very old, has been clipped or has health issues, he may need to wear a horse blanket (rug) in bad weather.

Something to eat all the time. Horses' stomachs are very different from ours. They have to be able to snack **all the time,** and should never be left without grass or hay. They can get very sore tummies if left without food for long spells, and may start to chew on fences or stables. This can cause serious health issues.

YOUR HORSE'S HOME

Even if your horse has a big stable, he will feel very lonely if he can't go out and socialise with equine friends. Make sure that if he is in a stable, he can still see his friends.

Most horses really like to be able to touch each other over a wall so they don't feel like they are in jail! Remember to muck out properly (don't just hide droppings under the bedding). Too much pee left in the bed will cause damage to your horse's lungs. Standing in poop and pee is gross, but can also seriously damage your horse's feet.

 What do you call a horse that lives next door to you? A neigh-bour!

Paddocks, fields & fencing

Horses were not meant to live in stables. Horses are designed to move all day over large distances. It is very good for horses to spend as much time as possible outside. Many horses live outside 24/7, and with food & shelter they are very happy & healthy.

Make sure the fencing around your horse's field is safe by checking it regularly. Keep all gates closed. Barbed wire is dangerous for horses and should be avoided.

Horse Life Crossword

Answer the questions below by filling in the blanks in the puzzle.

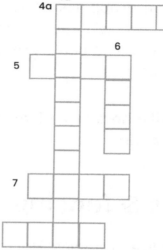

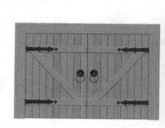

ACROSS

- 2a - a female foal
- 4a - a female person who is good with horses
- 5 - the gait in between walk and lope or canter
- 7 - half way up the horse's hind leg
- 8 - what the horse smells with

DOWN

- 1 - you sit on it when you ride
- 2d - a baby horse
- 3 - to get up onto a horse
- 4d - what horses wear on their feet sometimes
- 6 - Another name for the saddle and bridle

Answers: 2a filly, 4a horsewoman, 5 trot, 7 hock, 8 nose, 1 saddle, 2d foal, 3 mount, 4d horseshoes, 6 tack

FOOD + WATER

Horses mostly need grass, hay or haylage and should have these all the time. Horses graze at least 18 hours a day. Humans usually eat 3 meals a day, but horses need to snack **all day long**. In nature, wild horses also find weeds, herbs, leaves, berries and bark to eat.

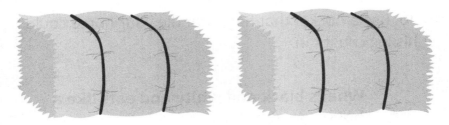

Your fields and hay may not have quite enough nutrition, so your horse may also need a little bit of feed balancer or some vitamins.

 A horse walks into a bar. "Hey," says the barman. "Yes please," says the horse.

If your horse does lots of exercise and gets thin, then add some horse feed like sugar beet, oats or horse and pony nuts to his diet. This is called hard feed, and should only be fed in small quantities.

 How do you spell 'Hungry Horse' in four letters? MTGG.

FOOD + WATER

Your horse must also always have fresh clean water, even in the field. Check the water bucket or trough at least once a day, and more often if it's hot outside.

Do not use a bucket that has a handle your horse could get his leg caught in.

 What's black and white and eats like a horse? A zebra.

Feeding rule: Feed little & often

 A horse is tied to a fifteen-foot rope and there is a bale of hay 25 feet away from him. The horse however is still able to eat from the hay. How is this possible? *The rope wasn't tied to anything.*

Each week take note of your horse's weight (you can use a weight tape for this). You do not want your horse to be either too fat or too skinny. Neither are good for their health. Be observant of your horse's body changes over time is very important for all horse people.

HELP THE HORSES FIND THEIR FOOD!

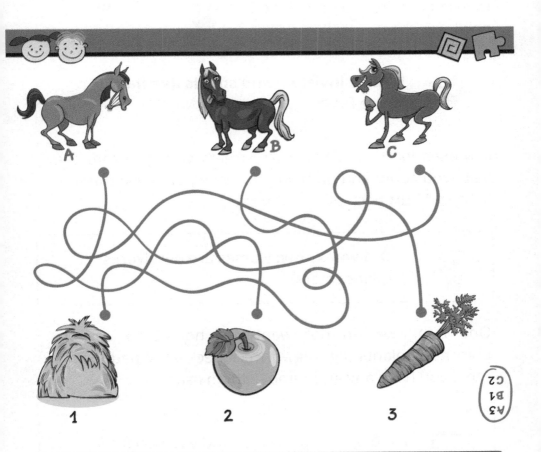

HORSE TREATS

Carrots are a healthy tasty treat. An occasional slice of apple is good too, but not too much! As a general rule, don't feed treats by hand as you can teach your horse to be pushy (not good). It's safer to put the treat on the ground or in a feed bowl.

 What's invisible and smells like hay?
Horse farts.

If horses learn that you carry treats with you into the field, you could end up being trampled, or cause them to fight and hurt each other for treats.

 Did you know: Horses are herbivores (plant eaters).

One thing we do not want our horses to eat are poisonous plants (eg. ragworth). Check your paddock to see if you have any and remove them asap.

 If a bag of apples is $3, and you bought 5 bags, how much change would you have from $20?

Answer: $5

CAN YOU FIND THE FIVE TYPES OF HORSE FOOD?

```
C  A  R  R  O  T  R  I  D  B
S  P  G  S  T  P  K  E  V  E
S  P  W  D  L  E  M  E  N  N
I  L  C  R  B  R  H  O  C  H
Q  E  F  O  A  T  S  B  V  E
H  R  C  A  L  I  C  O  G  R
A  O  L  Y  D  A  C  T  Y  B
Y  E  X  O  C  N  N  C  G  S
```

FIND THE HORSE FOOD QUIZ
Carrot, Apple, Hay, Oats, Herbs

IS YOUR HORSE SICK?

It is your job to look after your horse. Make sure you check him every day by looking him over thoroughly on both sides every day. Notice anything unusual. Often a horse may be sick, but it can be tricky for us to figure this out!

Signs that your horse may be sick:

- A horse that is **limping or lame.**
- **Not eating or drinking** is a sign that your horse might have a sore tummy, which is VERY serious for a horse.
- Any **unusual behaviour**, like being alone in the field instead of with his favourite buddy, or acting sleepy.
- **Coughing or a runny nose** with white, yellow or green snot. Clear snot is ok!
- **Panting and sweating at rest**, even when it's not hot outside.
- A **cut or blood** anywhere.
- Any **wounds.**
- **Lumps or swellings.**

Did you know: Horses with pink skin on their nose can get sunburnt.

If you see any signs that your horse might be sick, or even if you aren't sure but have a feeling he is just not right, you should always tell an adult who knows about horses. They can help you decide whether to call the vet, the farrier, the dentist or the physiotherapist.

HELP THE VET FIND THE SICK HORSE

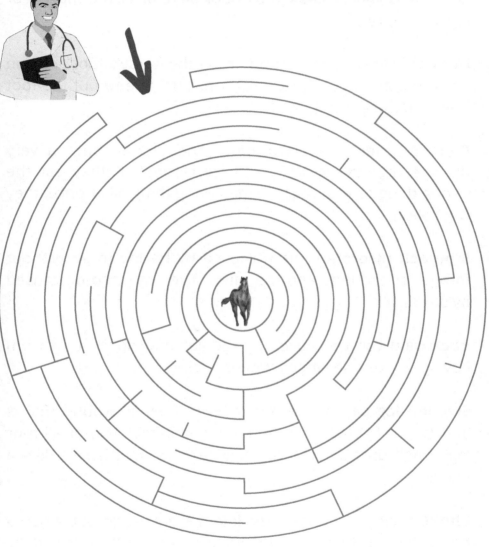

 Did you know: Horses can not vomit.

COMMON ILLNESSES IN HORSES

Lameness can be caused by hoof pain, or also a muscle or tendon injury.

Hoof abscess is an infection inside the horse's foot and can be so painful that a horse might not be able to put the foot down on the ground.

Colic is a very serious tummy ache. Horses have a very delicate digestive system and can't vomit. If they eat the wrong thing or too much of the wrong thing all at once, they can colic.

Stomach ulcers are often caused by having to go without forage for too long and too often. They can also be caused by stress.

Back pain can be caused by saddles that don't fit, or from having to exercise when a horse is lame.

Swollen leg can be caused by even a small wound that is infected or from a tendon injury. Sometimes two or all four legs swell up from too much time in a small space, like a stable.

Choke is when food gets stuck in the horse's throat, when a horse doesn't chew properly or eats something he shouldn't.

 Where do horses go when they're sick?
The horsepital.

COMMON ILLNESSES IN HORSES

Breathing allergies make it hard for your horse to breathe. Sometimes this is from plant pollen, but some horses are allergic to dust and need all their hay to be soaked.

Infectious diseases like flu and strangles can be passed from horse to horse especially when new horses are introduced to a group or at competitions.

 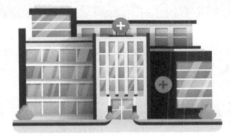 

Mud rash or mud fever is a horrible bacterial infection usually around the horse's heels from standing in the wet too long. It can also appear as rain scald along the horse's back, even under the rug.

Worms - If your horse isn't given a wormer regularly, worms can multiply and cause colic or ulcers.

 Did you know: Horses will usually not lie down together because at least one will act as a look-out to alert its friends of potential dangers.

What do you give a sick horse? A Cough stirrup

Sick Horse

WORD SCRAMBLE

GUESS THE WORD!

LICCO	
RUNNBUS	
MEAL	
GHOUC	
LUF	

 A pony went to the doctor complaining about having a sore throat. The doctor said: "It's OK, you're just a little horse."

Answers: Colic, sunburn, lame, cough, flu

GROOMING YOUR HORSE

Grooming your horse is a good way to check for cuts and scrapes and can help you to bond with your horse. You should always groom before tacking up or putting your horses rug on because otherwise, muddy areas on your horse's coat can cause sores.

Grooming should be enjoyable for your horse. If there are areas your horse doesn't like you to touch, try going back to an area on his body that he is happy with and then move more slowly towards the bit he didn't like.

Or maybe you need to be a bit more gentle. Maybe your horse prefers certain brushes to others. Grooming should be a happy and relaxing experience for both you and your horse.

Your horse should be happy to stand on a loose rope while you groom. This way your horse can move and communicate to you if anytime the grooming is uncomfortable for them.

If your horse is very unhappy about you grooming a particular area, he may be sore there. Then it would be a good idea to start investigating if he is in pain anywhere. Sometimes horses can have ulcers which you can't see, which might make them feel very uncomfortable.

GROOMING YOUR HORSE

Sweat scraper

Hoofpick

Body brush

Dandy brush

Curry comb

Water brush

Mane comb

The main tools you should have in your grooming kit are: a curry comb, a body brush, a dandy brush, two sponges (use one for the bottom and one for the face), a hoof pick, a hoof brush, a mane and tail comb or hairbrush.

Remember the most important tool of all: your hands!

Feel for lumps, bumps and scrapes with your fingers as you groom. You may not always see everything under all that hair, but your fingers will feel if there are clumps of mud or maybe a scab or cut.

GROOMING KIT MAZES

Find the grooming brush in each maze.

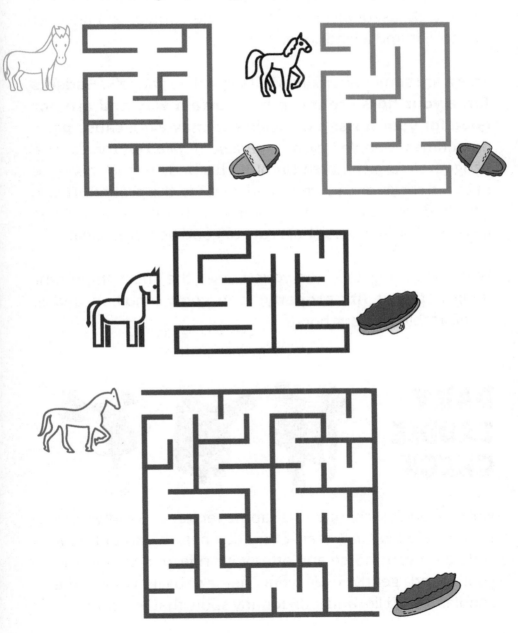

HORSE TRAINING EQUIPMENT

The training equipment used with horses is called tack. The main tack used includes the saddle, bridle, a halter or headcollar and a lead rope.

There are some other kinds of tack, called gadgets. **Gadgets force your horse to move in a certain way and are not good for your horse's muscles and may even cause pain.** Sometimes people *(even experienced people)* try to use gadgets to force a horse to round his body or tuck his nose in to his chest, or carry his head lower to the ground. This is very bad for your horse's health and should be avoided at all costs. There are no short cuts to good horsemanship.

When choosing tack for your horse, the most important thing is that it **fits properly**, is in good condition and is comfortable for your horse.

DAILY SADDLE CHECK

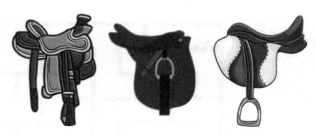

Horse's bodies change in shape over time. Saddles can also develop wear & tear. Every day before you put your saddle on your horse and after your ride, you should run your hand gently over your horse's back where the saddles would lie, and look for any spots that are sore.

HORSE TRAINING QUIZ

1: The thing you sit on when you ride a horse is called a:

    a: Rug
    b: Curry comb
    c: Saddle
    d: Halter

2: Gadgets are:

    a: Tack that forces a horse to move in a certain way
    b: A part of the bridle
    c: A type of girth
    d: A great idea!

3: The most important thing when choosing tack for a horse is:

    a: That the colours match my horse
    b: That they are really expensive
    c: That the bridle and saddle are the same colour
    d: That they fit really comfortably

4: If your horse starts behaving oddly when you ride, you must always check this to see if this is hurting your horse's back:

    a: Your riding hat
    b: Your saddle
    c: Your stable
    d: Your coat

Answers: 1c, 2a, 3d, 4b

HORSE MATHS

Count the number of items:

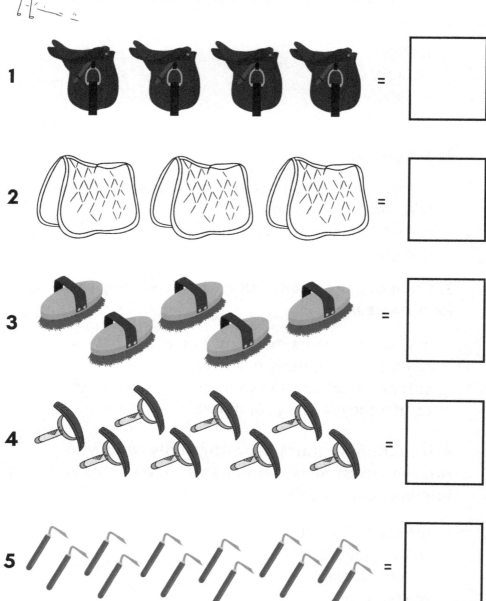

1 =

2 =

3 =

4 =

5 =

SADDLES

There are lots of different types of saddles: English (dressage, jumping or general purpose), western, racing, treeless, endurance, stock and many more. The most important thing is that the saddle is comfortable for you and your horse, and is suitable for what you and your horse want to do.

YOUR PERFECT SADDLE:

- Should fit your horse.
- Should fit your weight & height and you should feel comfortable and confident when riding. The saddle should not be too big or small for you. *It's quite hard to find the perfect saddle to fit your & your horse!*
- Your legs and knees should not get sore when you ride.
- Should not slip left or right on the horse.
- Should not slip up the horse's neck or backwards.
- It should not be too long on your horse's back (can make your horse's back sore)
- It should be the correct width for your horse - not too narrow and not too wide (both are bad!).
- When you ride the saddle should naturally put you in a position where you can draw a line from your shoulder to your hip to your heel.

 What is a horses favorite state? Neighbraska.

Parts of the bridle

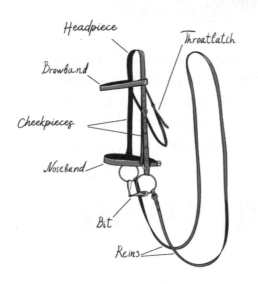

Headpiece
Throatlatch
Browband
Cheekpieces
Noseband
Bit
Reins

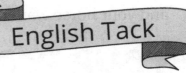

English Tack

Parts of the saddle

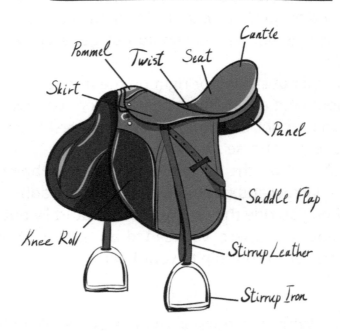

Pommel
Twist
Seat
Cantle
Skirt
Panel
Saddle Flap
Knee Roll
Stirrup Leather
Stirrup Iron

BRIDLES + HALTERS

Just like with saddles, there are also lots of different types of bridles. The bridle and reins help you to communicate with the horse using tiny messages from your fingers. You will learn how to ride well enough not to pull on the reins so you don't hurt your horse's mouth. Many great riders can ride without using a bridle at all!

There are so many types of bits out there, and each horse has a different mouth shape. So putting the wrong bit into a horse's mouth is a common problem around the world. Some horses, because of where their teeth have grown, should NEVER use a bit at all, as it will always bang on their teeth while you ride. Ouch!

"Great riders have very sensitive and light hands. They can use all of their fingers independently to communicate to the horse subtly, and it becomes like a beautiful dance"

When using a bridle, choose one that has a simple noseband that does not tie the horse's mouth closed. These are common in some areas, but they can cause the horse to hold tension in their mouth, and can make it tricky to swallow and yawn. Most bridles can be used with no noseband at all.

Bridles and halters need to fit comfortably and not be too tight or too loose.

BITLESS BRIDLES

Bitless bridles

Some bridles, like hackamores from California (bosal & mecate) & other bitless bridles, don't have bits! Bits are not always needed when you ride a horse. In fact many horses are happier and ride better without a bit in their mouth.

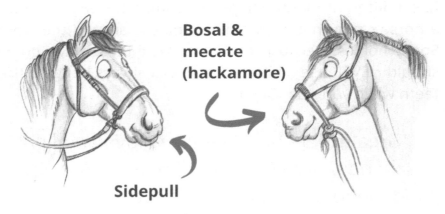

Bosal & mecate (hackamore)

Sidepull

The rope halter is mostly used for groundwork, but lots of riders who have trained their horses well use a halter instead of a bridle to ride too.

Bridles and halters need to fit comfortably and not be too tight or too loose.

On all bridles and halters, the noseband should be about half way between the top of the nostril & the eye. If the noseband is too low, it can make it difficult for your horse to breathe.

Parts of the western bridle

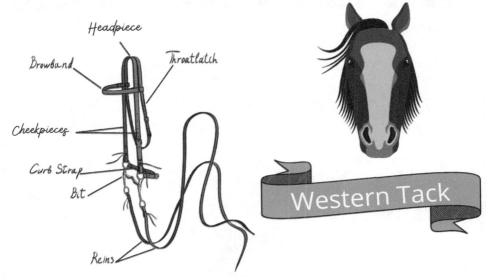

Headpiece

Browband

Throatlatch

Cheekpieces

Curb Strap

Bit

Reins

Western Tack

Parts of the western saddle

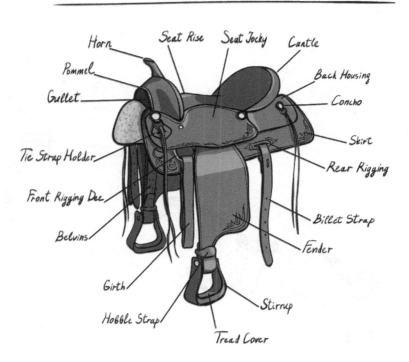

Horn

Seat Rise

Seat Jocky

Cantle

Pommel

Back Housing

Gullet

Concho

Tie Strap Holder

Skirt

Front Rigging Dee

Rear Rigging

Belvins

Billet Strap

Girth

Fender

Hobble Strap

Stirrup

Tread Cover

MAZE! FIND THE LOST SADDLE

Start here

HORSE EQUIPMENT

E	Y	E	S	H	A	B
N	E	A	G	A	E	R
S	A	D	D	L	E	I
Y	G	I	R	T	H	D
E	O	O	I	E	A	L
B	I	T	T	R	F	E

Find 5 pieces of horse training equipment

Answers: Saddle, bit, bridle, girth, halter

HORSE MATH PUZZLE

When Chester the horse was 8, his brother was half his age. Now, Chester the horse is 14. How old is his brother?

Answer: His brother is 10. Half of 8 is 4, so Chester the horse's brother is 4 years younger. This means when Chester the horse is 14, his brother is still 4 years younger, so he's 10.

CLEANING YOUR TACK

You need to look after your tack and clean it often so it stays soft for your horse and doesn't cause rubs or sores. Tack that gets too stiff can also wear out, crack and tear which will make it very unsafe.

Clean your bridle and girth after every ride, even if you just wipe your horse's sweat off. You should also wash the bit with clean water after every ride.

For a proper clean, at least once a week, or every time it gets muddy, clean all your tack with saddle soap, saddle oil and clean water. Always keep your tack somewhere dry and safe.

SAFETY

Always remember that horses can move very quickly and suddenly if they are startled. They are big and can hurt you very badly without meaning to. You may not always see or hear what they do. Until you are very experienced, you should always make sure you have an adult around when you are near horses.

Horses have their eyes at the sides of their face, which means they can see very well all around them, except right in front and right behind them. **Try to always approach horses from the side, so they can see you coming.** Although they prefer quiet to shouting, make sure they can hear you when you are behind them by talking to them. Never sneak up on a horse.

Safety when riding

- Wear a hard riding hat to protect your head in case you fall off.
- Wear boots with a small heel, to keep your feet from slipping through the stirrups

Safety on the ground

- Wear a hard riding hat to protect your head.
- Be able to lead your horse from both sides (left and right).
- Never wrap your lead rope around your hand. Instead, fold the rope so the rope is easy to let go if you need to.

HORSE SAFETY QUIZ

1: A horse that you love will never hurt you because he loves you too.

   a: True
   b: False

2: You should always have an adult nearby when you are near horses unless you are very experienced.

   a: True
   b: False

3: Even a horse that is very well trained and knows you well may get startled and move very suddenly.

   a: True
   b: False

4: The best way to approach a horse is to sneak up quietly, right behind him and then yell loudly to let him know where you are.

   a: True
   b: False

5: At what age will you know everything there is to know about horses?

   a: 18
   b: 45
   c: 80
   d: You will never know it all

Answers: 1b, 2a, 3a, 4b, 5d

RIDING + TRAINING HORSES

Horses are not born knowing how to be ridden. This is something they have to be taught. A horse who is shown how to be handled and ridden in a kind way will be happy with someone riding them. Before horses are taught to be ridden, it is very important that they are trained to understand lots of other things too.

Leaving their herd for short times, having their feet picked up, leading politely and learning to be touched and groomed are all things that need to be taught with patience, kindness and understanding. A few months before you want to have your horse happy to have a rider on board, you need to start your preparations. This could include:

- **Getting used to going new places**, by leading your horse in hand for a few miles each week. Every horse should do this before they start riding. This helps the horse become very confident & safer to ride.
- **Increasing confidence.** Showing your horse the tack you will use in the future. Making noises with the cinch or girth. Making noises with the stirrups. Putting the numnah or saddle blanket on your horse's back.
- **Simple groundwork lessons** in just a halter on the ground, like going forwards, turning right, turning left & walking backwards.
- **Being happy & confident** around people and not being scared or worried.
- **Take your time.** All of this is done *before* anyone sits on the horse for the first time. This part of the process usually takes a few months, and is well worth it. Good horse training is slow, and requires time & patience to do it right.

It's very important that horses are not ridden until they are at least 4 years old. This is because they have to grow so their bones and muscles are strong enough. When horses are ridden too much when they are too young, it can cause them pain and health issues later in their lives. Just because they are big and can run fast, doesn't always mean their bones and muscles are strong enough to carry a rider.

 Did you know: Horses use their ears, eyes and nostrils to express their mood. They also communicate their feelings through facial expressions.

Not all horses' bones finish growing at exactly the same age. This depends on their size and breed, and happens between the ages of 5.5 years at the earliest and sometimes even up to 8 years.

To keep horses healthy, you also need to understand that it takes time for horses to become and keep fit. So even a horse that is old enough to carry a rider needs to start a little bit at a time. If your horse has had a long holiday or time off because of sickness, it will take time to build up his strength and fitness again too.

 What did the mother horse say to her child horse? "It's hay pasture bedtime!"

Training Horses

WORD SCRAMBLE

GUESS THE WORD!

GINDIR

ORKOUDNGRW

NECIEPAT

CENCEFIDON

MEIT

What did the horse say when it fell?
"I've fallen and I can't giddyup!"

Answers: Riding, groundwork, patience, confidence, time

GROUNDWORK

Groundwork is everything you do with your horse, when you are not riding. It is very important. Groundwork a great way to practice communicating, build confidence, teach your horse exercises and prepare for ridden work. Nearly everything your horse needs to be able to do when you are riding, you should teach him on the ground first.

 Did you know: Horsemanship is not only about riding!

Groundwork is used to teach your horse to lead and walk, trot, canter, slow down, stop & turn. It doesn't always mean lunging in circles all the time. That would be really boring, and might even strain his bones and muscles. Groundwork can be done by going on walks, and exploring new things.

Another way to do groundwork is *without* a halter or rope. This is called **working at liberty**. This is a good way to test how well you can communicate with your horse without any equipment.

Remember the approach and retreat exercise?

Liberty work starts with that. See what happens when you turn your horse loose in the arena.

- Can you get him to follow you or does he just want to roll and look for grass at the fence?
- Can you get him to turn?
- Can you get him to walk with you in every direction, over poles?

GROUNDWORK

The most important thing in groundwork is that your horse is confident and relaxed. Your leadrope should always have a smile in it, so you know neither you or the horse are pulling.

You should always be patient, consistent and kind. That means that if things aren't working the way you want, you have to think about whether your horse really understands what you are asking. Are you being clear? Does your horse know the answer? You may need help with this, so try and have lessons from good instructors, or find good videos to watch so you can learn.

Remember, always end on a happy note and leave your horse wanting to do more. This means that even if you have made some mistakes, find something to do that your horse likes and enjoys to make sure you finish by having fun. Another good thing is to stop asking for more once your horse has figured out something that he found difficult. By stopping you are rewarding him and telling him he did the right thing.

FIND 2 SAME PICTURES

FEEL, TIMING + BALANCE

Being a good horse person is not about asking your horse to do certain things. It's also about:

- Never calling a horse disrespectful or naughty. Horses are honest. But we can confuse them when we ask them new things.
- Asking your horse the right question at the right time.
- Asking with a small cue, and not shouting at your horse or kicking them with your legs if you are riding, and never losing your temper or feeling angry.
- Stop asking the *second* your horse is thinking of the right answer. Often this can be before they even move a step! Ask how you can 'help' your horse, and not 'make' your horse do things.

HANDWRITING CHALLENGE

Trace the upper case letters of these groundwork exercises.

POLES

WALK

GROOM

LIBERTY

HORSE TRAINING

Every time we are with a horse we are training them. Even just leading them to the paddock, or when we are picking out their feet!

Horses learn that they have done the right thing when you release the pressure and stop asking. *What that means is that when you are leading your horse and he dives down to graze, you really must not allow it because you are teaching him that diving down for grass is what you want him to do!*

If your horse pulls his foot out of your hands every time you try to pick his feet, try to hold on until he stops pulling. Then, as soon as he stops, praise him and put his foot down. The next time, see if he can let you hold his foot a second or two longer, and so on. Soon you will be able to pick out his feet properly.

Remember, safety first! If your horse is really pulling you around and you feel out of control, always ask an adult to help you.

Horses are never deliberately naughty. They simply learn what works for them to get what they want. Your job is to find out what that is, and figure out how to get your horse to want the same thing as you. When you can do that, you're becoming a smart horsemanship trainer!

 Did you know: A horse will always be 100% honest. Horses never lie.

TRUE OR FALSE QUIZ

1: A good horse trainer can force a horse to do what she wants even if the horse is really scared.

  a: True
  b: False

2: A good horse trainer will find a way to help a horse feel confident about things that worry him.

  a: True
  b: False

3: The best way to teach a horse to stop being naughty is to punish bad behaviour.

  a: True
  b: False

4: Groundwork is a way of exercising a horse in circles for long periods of time until he gets too tired to be naughty.

  a: True
  b: False

5: Taking a horse for a walk is a form of groundwork that can be a fun way of building a partnership.

  a: True
  b: False

Answers: 1b, 2a, 3b, 4b, 5a

HORSE RIDING CLOTHES

 How does a horse from Kentucky greet another horse? With Southern Horsepitality!

The main things you need to wear when you ride are riding boots with a heel that stops your foot from sliding through the stirrup and a hard riding hat. You may also want to wear breeches or leggings if jeans are uncomfortable.

It does not matter how much your clothes cost, as long as they are safe and comfortable & do the job. Your horse will never care how much money you spent on brand name clothes!

 What's the hardest thing about learning to ride a horse? The ground!

HOLDING THE REINS

Hold the reins as gently as if you are holding an ice cream cone.

HORSE RIDING CROSSWORD

ACROSS

3. A female foal
4. Another word for horse, or about horses
7. The top part of a horse's back leg
8. A male foal
10. A female horse

DOWN

1 What straps the saddle onto the horse?
2. What does the horse wear on his head for ridden work?
5. What has 7 cervical bones?
6. A small fenced field
9. When your horse limps, he's

_____

MOUNTING BLOCK

Your horse will thank you for using a mounting block to mount instead of from the ground. When you pull yourself up into the saddle from the ground, the saddle really pulls on your horse's back.

If this happens often, he may even need a physiotherapist!

Even when you use a mounting block, be gentle when you get on. Make sure you don't dig into your horse's side with your toes, and don't bump him in the hindquarters with your other foot as you swing your leg over. Sit down gently into the saddle, don't just drop your weight down suddenly

How to dismount

How you dismount is important too. Make sure your horse is standing still. Take your feet out of both stirrups. Hold the reins in your left hand and keep it on the front of the saddle. Bend forward at the waist and swing your right leg behind and over (without bumping your horse's hindquarters) and slide down gently until your feet are on the ground.

Lead line

The pony usually stays on a lead line until we can are properly balanced as we ride and not relying on the reins for balance. It depends on your teacher, but they will make sure you are safe at a walk at least before taking the lead line off.

HORSE RIDING

Learning to ride a horse never stops. Even the best riders are still learning and have lessons! Every new horse-human partnership means learning how to communicate all over again. However, in the beginning, when you are learning the very basics, riding is about the mechanics of learning how to sit and keep your balance without hanging on to the reins while someone leads your horse for you. Once you find your balance, you will learn how to turn, stop, and walk on. You will learn how to use your seat, hands and legs, and how to hold the reins. Always try to remember, no matter what, that you are sitting on a living, breathing creature. Your horse feels everything you do up there!

"With a really good rider, no one can actually see what they are doing, or how they are asking their horse to do things. Their body is relaxed & moves very little. It looks like a beautiful dance with a happy horse."

- Always look where you are going (not at your horse's head).
- Don't pull on the reins. Use gentle hands and never hurt your horse's mouth.
- Smile & breathe. It's meant to be fun!
- Every time your fingers move a tiny fraction on the reins you are sending a message to your horse.

"A great horse person needs 3 things: The head, the heart and the hands"

HORSE RIDING

 Why was the horse really proud of his school test results? Because he got an Hay-plus!

Once you are able to walk, stop, and turn your horse to the left and right and use your reins, seat and legs; smile and breathe! You're ready to try your first trot.

When you get used to how bouncy it feels and get the hang of rising and sitting trot, it all magically becomes a lot more manageable! Then you will have your first canter.

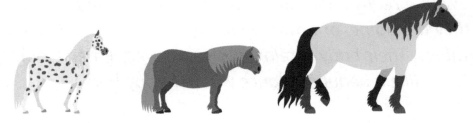

None of this can be learned from a book. You will need lots and lots of lessons from a kind and patient instructor on a steady and patient horse.

 A woman rode her horse all the way up a hill on Friday. The next day she rode back on Friday, too. How is this possible? The horse is called Friday.

WALK, TROT + CANTER

The walk is a four-beat gait. What that means is that for each stride, you will have all four feet lift and land separately. Can you feel each of these feet land and know which ones they are without looking?

The trot is a two-beat gait. For each stride, two (the front right with the hind left, or the other opposite pair) feet lift and land. See if you can feel which ones are doing this as you ride the trot.

The canter is a three beat gait. First the outside hind foot lands and pushes the horse's body (and you) up, then the inside hind and outside front feet land together, then the inside front lands.

 Which side of the horse has the most hair?
The outside!

Learning to feel and then to influence how each foot moves can take a long time and loads of practice. Great riders know how to do this without even thinking about it. Have you ever watched a reining horse do a spin? Imagine sitting on that and still being able to know which feet are doing what!

The horse

WORD SCRAMBLE

GUESS THE WORD!

DELDSA

DELRIB

RETCAN

GINDELG

RAME

Answers: Saddle, bridle, canter, gelding, mane

A woman buys a horse for $40. She sells the horse for $60. She then buys the horse back for $80. And she sells the horse again for $85. In the end, how much money did she make or lose? Or did she break even?

Answers She made $25

GOOD HORSEMANSHIP

Good horsemanship doesn't mean you have to be the best rider or trainer. **It does mean considering your horse's feelings every time you are with him.**

When you are learning to ride try to always remember that a horse can feel a fly landing on his back, so he can feel everything you do. It's really hard to learn a new skill and be gentle at the same time, but you need to try.

When you want to go faster, instead of suddenly kicking your horse hard, try *thinking* of moving faster first, and increasing the energy you are feeling in your body.

Imagine the ice cream shop is giving away free ice cream! Feel that excitement in your body, and your horse will feel it too.

If that isn't enough, then try a gentle nudge with your legs. **Then, as soon as your horse does move faster, stop asking!**

 What sort of horses come out after dark?
Nightmares

Horses know they have done the right thing when you stop asking. **Always remember to thank your horse too.**

The goal is to get your horse to respond to the smallest ask. When you get very good at communicating with your horse, he will understand your thoughts!

HORSE RIDING + BEING SICK

Sometimes when you are riding you may wonder if your horse is feeling well.

If your horse feels lame, or is acting strangely, try and find out what the problem is before continuing. You may want to get off and check his feet or do a little groundwork to see if you can spot something.

Other problems you may run into when you ride horses are bucking or bolting, or a horse that won't let you put on the saddle or bridle.

Safety is the most important thing, so ask an adult for help. Quite often strange behaviour by the horse means your horse is telling you something is sore or he is feeling sick.

 Why did the horse eat with its mouth open? Because he had bad stable manners.

HORSE RIDING QUIZ

1: The trot is

    a: A three-beat gait
    b: A two-beat gait
    c: A kind of bit
    d: A kind of saddle

2: The most important clothing for riding is

    a: A hard hat and riding boots with a heel that stops your foot from sliding through the stirrup
    b: A cowboy hat and bandana to keep dust out of your nose
    c: Spurs
    d: Breeches and a show jacket

3: The canter is

    a: A part of the saddle
    b: A four-beat gait
    c: The slowest gait
    d: A three-beat gait

4: If I want my horse to go faster when I'm riding I should

    a: Shout "Giddy-up!"
    b: Look ahead, think forwards & increase the energy in my body
    c: Kick hard three times
    d: Lean back and slap my horse's backside

Answers: 1b, 2a, 3d, 4b

CONCLUSION

The best thing about loving horses is knowing that riding is only a small part of being with them. Horses are amazing, powerful, beautiful and intelligent animals that just want to get along with everyone and feel safe.

When you learn how to communicate with them and to understand what matters to them, you will also learn the importance of patience.

Horses don't care about rosettes or winning competitions. They care about kindness and fairness. Anyone can learn how to ride. To some it comes naturally, and for others it takes a lot more practice. It takes thousands of hours to learn to ride well.

However, only a true horseman or horsewoman, will learn to enjoy the process of building a real connection with a horse. The connection is what matters the most, and it has nothing to do with riding.

 What kind of horse can swim underwater?
A seahorse

And never forget, it's all about listening to the horse.

Name _____

MY PONY

Complete the story using the writing prompt below.

When I have a pony _____

_____

_____

_____

_____

_____

_____

_____

_____

_____

_____

_____

_____

_____

PONY SAVINGS TRACKER

SAVING FOR _____ AMOUNT _____ DUE BY _____

DATE	AMOUNT SAVED	BALANCE
	TOTAL SAVINGS	

Congratulations! You are on your way to becoming an amazing horse person. I would be very grateful if you could share your review & a picture of this book online. Thank you.

LESSONS I LEARNED FROM THIS BOOK:

_____

_____

_____

_____

_____

_____

_____

_____

_____

_____

THE CORAL COVE SERIES

www.writtenbyelaine.com

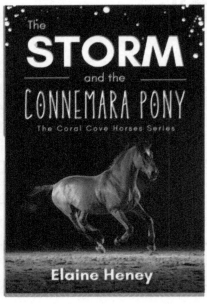

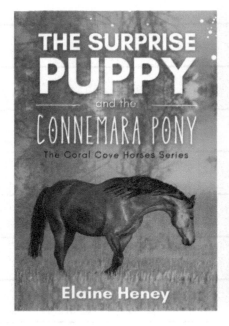

THE
CONNEMARA
ADVENTURE SERIES
FOR KIDS 8+

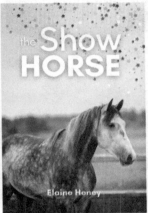

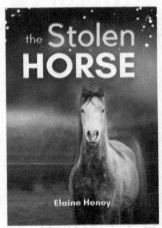

HORSE BOOKS
by #1 best-selling author
ELAINE HENEY

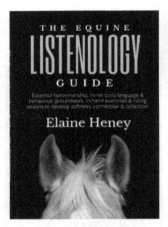
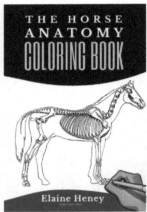

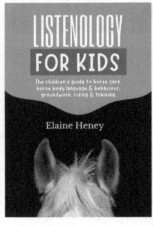
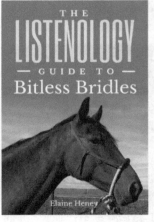

www.elaineheneybooks.com

Made in the USA
Las Vegas, NV
24 November 2023

81373696R10056